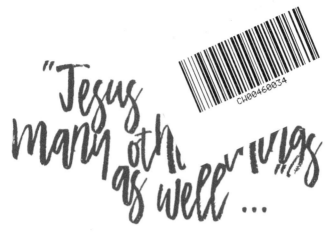

"Jesus many other things as well ...

BOOK TWO

"Jesus did many other things as well ..."

BOOK TWO

more

SHORT STORIES OUT OF JAPAN

TONY & PAT SCHMIDT

CONTENTS

PREFACE

Some of you may have read my first book *Jesus did many other things as well…: short stories out of Japan.* They are stories of some of the things that God did during our 33 years as foreign missionaries in Japan, in spite of our many short-comings.

After that book was published, I felt humbled by the many requests for "more stories." This time my wife Pat joined me, adding some of her stories too.

Like the first book, this book is also stories of what God did and of how He has worked in people's lives. They are stories of how God patiently taught us and helped us to better understand the world of Japan and her people as we shared the Gospel.

As in the first book, all the stories are true, but names have been changed to protect the identity of those involved.

Special thanks again to our insightful good friends, Rose Carleton and Bless Ho, who proofread and edited the stories. Rose, Bless, the Chinese translator of the first book— Dr Max Hui, and Dr Enoch and Becky Wong graciously encouraged us to move forward with this project. Without their support and encouragement, we would probably not have persevered. We are also very grateful to our publishers, Siretona Creative for their expertise and invaluable help.

If you have a heart to reach Japanese people for Christ, we hope these stories will encourage you. No matter where we are on the journey of life, we can all learn from the lessons He teaches each one of us.

Tony and Pat Schmidt
Vancouver, Canada, August 2023

1. WHAT ABOUT MY PARENTS?

Pat

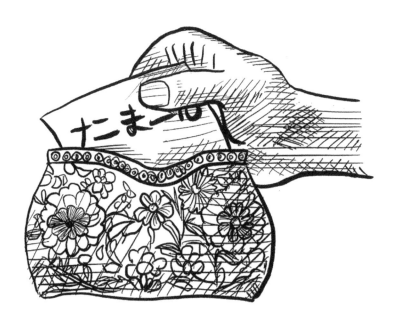

*Honor your father and your mother, so that you may live long
in the land the LORD your God is giving you.*
- Exodus 20:12

Although I, Pat, did not grow up as a PK (preacher's kid), by the time God called Tony and me to be missionaries in Japan my Dad had become a pastor. At first my parents were quite supportive of our going to Japan, but I later realized that this was because we had only initially signed up for four years. When God called us into long-term service, suddenly my parents were quite resistant.

Many parents, even some Christian parents, struggle with the call that God puts on their children's lives. Many children struggle with feelings of guilt over leaving their parents. In my parents' case I don't think they were against our leaving them. They themselves had immigrated to South Africa from Holland when they were quite young, so I found it very distressing when they said things like, "We don't think that missionaries are needed in Japan anymore." I thought they would be pleased that their daughter was obeying God's call on her life. It was mystifying!

Later I thought that possibly my parents found it difficult to send me to Japan because so many of their relatives and countrymen living in Indonesia had been killed and cruelly treated by the Japanese during the Second World War.

Whatever the reason for their resistance, once they came to visit us in Japan they changed completely. God gave them

His eyes to see that the Japanese people need the Gospel – just as people all over the world do. The Japanese are lost without Jesus, just as we all are before we receive Him as our Lord and Savior.

I remember my Dad being fascinated by the way Mrs. Tanaka sat so quietly with a sweet half-smile on her face as she and her husband sat on cushions on the floor when visiting us in our home. "Whatever was she thinking?" asked my Dad after they left. "Oh," I said, "she was no doubt thinking a lot! She is a very smart lady, and a wonderful Christian."

Mrs. Tanaka was indeed a remarkable woman. She was studying at university when she met her husband. He fell in love with her and asked her to marry him. She refused, saying she had already decided what she was going to do with her life. She wanted to study to get her master's degree to work with people who had physical and mental disabilities. Mr. Tanaka wasn't to be dissuaded, however. He promised that if she married him, he would let her go back to university after she raised their children. When their youngest daughter was just nine, we worked with them to establish a church in the south of Sapporo. When the children were all grown, true to his word, Mr. Tanaka encouraged her to get her master's degree. She did, and together they began a wonderful work for people with physical and mental disabilities – but that's another story...

After that first visit to Japan, my parents enthusiastically supported us through prayer, encouragement and finances. My Mom wrote faithfully every week. Once she wrote to say she had found a little piece of paper in her purse that said "Tamago 10" and wondered if it was important? Tony and I had a good laugh. Tamago means eggs in Japanese. When they were in Japan they sometimes they went off to the local store to buy eggs for us, armed with sufficient Japanese to make the purchase. They were so proud of us and never once said, "If only you would come back to South Africa." God had changed their hearts.

Once my parents got into their 80's, I promised to try to see them every two years. As they got older and frailer, we felt the separation more deeply. However, they were in a good living situation in South Africa and they still had each other. When my mother was called Home at the age of 89, I told my father that I would go to South Africa to look after him. He flatly refused, saying that Mom would have had none of it! They had sent us to Japan to tell the Japanese about Jesus, and that hadn't changed. I was amazed to see how strong God's call was on his life too!

My father's physical condition slowly weakened and he kept saying, "I saw Mom off, so now there is nothing more for me to do. I am ready to go. Nowadays I wake up in the morning surprised I am still here, and I ask the Lord why He hasn't taken me Home." However, God still had some important truths to teach both him and me.

Dad was adamant that he didn't want to go to a care facility. He had often visited the patients there and found that many of them could not carry on a conversation. He wanted to stay in his own home, and that was that! He could be very stubborn.

In those days I phoned my father quite often from Japan just to chat. One day I phoned three times and there was no answer. As I knew he wouldn't be out, I was concerned. I emailed a friend of my parents and asked her to check on him.

She emailed back to say that she had found my father standing in a room in a care facility where he had been taken. He had fallen in his home and was found in very poor condition. Dad, stubborn as ever, refused to get into the bed at the care home, insisting that he wanted to go home.

When I received this news, I asked the Lord what I could say to Dad that would help him. God brought to my mind Paul's words in Colossians 1:27, "Christ in you, the hope of glory."

I sent a quick email to my parents' friend for her to pass on to my father. I wrote, "Dad, if you really believe these words, and I know you do, the place where you are doesn't really matter, does it? Christ is in you – that's your hope of glory." My Dad read that and somehow it struck a chord in his heart. God's Word spoke to God's child. My Dad quietly submitted to the care facility staff and cooperated.

Two days later God called my father Home. How wonderful that he could go to his Heavenly Father agreeing that He is in control of all our circumstances. God does what is best for us all.

Are you a parent who is struggling with the fact that God is calling your precious child or grandchild to serve Him in another country? We pray that you will be blessed in taking up their call as your own. God will reward you in His own wonderful way.

When God calls us, He calls our children too. It was my blessed experience that when God called us to Japan, He also called my parents.

2. WHEN GOD CALLS, HE CALLS THE CHILDREN TOO

Pat

"I tell you the truth," Jesus replied, "no one who has left home or brothers or sisters or mother or father or children or fields for me and the gospel will fail to receive a hundred times as much in this present age (homes, brothers, sisters, mothers, children and fields — and with them, persecutions) and in the age to come, eternal life"
- Mark 10:29-30

Often we are asked the question, "What were your challenges in bringing up your children on the mission field?" It is our sure conviction that when God calls a couple to bring the Gospel to another country, He calls their children too. We also hear people say, "It's OK for you, but what about the children? It's not their choice to live in another country. It's yours!" But that is not true. When God calls, it is not our choice but His, and He calls the whole family.

Having said that, there were some big issues we had to face. It was hard to see our two boys struggle with being the only Caucasians in their schools and neighborhood. They did not like the extra attention, whereas our daughter quite enjoyed being treated like someone special! One day we passed a park with a very interesting playground. We stopped the car and asked the kids if they would like to play there. They all shouted an enthusiastic "Yes!" Then the boys looked at each other and said, "No. Let's go home to the park near us."

We knew it was because they suddenly remembered that if they played at this park they would soon have an entourage of other kids coming after them saying *"gaijin, gaijin"* (foreigner, foreigner). The Japanese children were not being mean – it was just so unusual for them to see a Caucasian child that it was their natural response. So we all went home. At our neighborhood park our children were accepted as local children. Their Japanese was excellent, and none of their friends thought of them as being foreigners.

One day as I, Pat, was going for a walk with our seven-year-old son through the park near our home, he bumped into a school friend. "Hey, Brad, did you make that dragon yet?" he asked. A conversation ensued, but I was thinking, *Why a dragon?* When we came home I asked Brad about it. He said they were doing a craft at school during art class, using large cardboard boxes. They had been instructed to make an *omikoshi* (a portable shrine to carry the Shinto gods), and Brad had to make a dragon to decorate it. Tony and I were very uncomfortable with that and eventually, after talking with Brad, we decided to phone the school. We said we were sorry, but we would not be sending Brad to school the next day, as we were a Christian family and were not happy with our child making a shrine for the Shinto gods. Strictly speaking, Japanese schools are not allowed to do religious activities in the schools, but many Japanese see these as cultural rather than religious activities.

That afternoon there was a knock on our door. It was a teacher from the school. We were expecting a scolding, but instead we got a wonderful surprise. The teacher explained that he was a Christian, but had never had the courage to say so to his colleagues. However, our request to keep our child out of school because of a "religious" activity caused such a stir in the staffroom that he finally stood up and said that he too was a Christian, and he would not want his children to make a Shinto shrine either. Then, with a huge smile on his face, he said, "Thank you! You gave me the opportunity to testify before my colleagues. I feel so happy about that. Now God can use me in that school!"

Being Caucasian also meant that everything we did was seen by all. One day we came home to find a couch on our doorstep. Our six- and seven-year-old sons excitedly said they had found it with the garbage to be collected. Being good missionary kids accustomed to frugal living, they had carried it home between the two of them. We could just imagine the stories that were going around as these two little foreign boys carried the couch from the garbage corner down the street to our house!

We found that the Japanese elementary schools offered an excellent education. The children all learned to read music. They learned to clean their classrooms themselves – not leaving it to the cleaning staff. They learned to serve food in a hygienic way as they took turns to serve the school lunches, starting in grade one. And they had excellent math teachers. All three of our children were ahead of their South African and Canadian counterparts in mathematics.

However, the move between countries proved to be a challenge each time. One year when we returned to South Africa and our second son was in grade four, it seemed that the change was too much for him. He became difficult to manage and had us all walking on eggshells. We decided to cut him some slack as we could understand how difficult it was for him to adjust. However, things just got worse. Finally, we cried out to the Lord for wisdom. This clear thought from the Lord came to us: *You have made it worse by moving the boundaries. What was considered as being rude to his parents is now acceptable. What was not an acceptable way of speaking to his siblings is now acceptable. Go back to what you know is right, and set up the boundaries again.*

That night we apologized to our son for letting him get away with his bad behavior! We told him that God had reprimanded us. He was not sure if he was happy with such an apology, but as soon as we returned to "normal" – where right was right and wrong was still wrong – Greg settled down and we had a happier home.

Even though our children now look back with gratitude on their experiences of moving from one culture to another, one school system to another, there certainly were difficult times. In 1994, South Africans all over the world were allowed to vote in the first democratic elections from wherever they were living. We stood with our oldest son in a long line of South Africans in Vancouver, Canada, waiting for our turn to vote. Suddenly Brad turned to us and said, "I feel weird – am I South African? Am I Japanese? Am I Canadian? What am I?" It was the struggle of identity that so many third culture kids experience. Fortunately the Lord gave us just the right words to say: "We are blessed more than most people – we belong to them all!"

Are you hesitating to do what you feel the Lord wants you to do because of your concern for your children? Know that He has remembered them, and He will enrich their lives as you follow Him.

3. MORE THAN WE CAN IMAGINE

Tony

God can do immeasurably more than all we ask or imagine.
- Ephesians 3:20

The Bible teaches that without faith we cannot please God. Yet even faith the "size of a mustard seed" moves the heart of God. Even very little faith brings forth the Lord's blessing. A father once asked Jesus to heal his son, adding "if you can." Jesus answered by saying that anything is possible to those who believe. "I do believe. Help me overcome my unbelief!" the father cried out, acknowledging his own weak faith. Jesus responded to his weak faith by healing his son (Mark 9:19-29).

I have been both joyfully surprised and embarrassingly ashamed at the quality of my own faith on several occasions while working as a missionary in Japan. Sometimes I even wondered if our supporters would continue to support us if they knew how weak my faith so often was. However, God is faithful and kind, and He firmly leads us on to trust Him more and more.

During the time we were leading a new church plant on the outskirts of Sapporo, the Lord gave us some unique experiences that strengthened my faith. Pat and I had moved into the area, enrolled our three children in the local Japanese school and kindergarten, and begun to get acquainted with our neighbors. Through the distribution of flyers, and through the many contacts our children made, the neighborhood became aware that a foreign Christian family had come to live amongst them. We started English classes, Sunday school and Bible studies. The work began without any Japanese believers, but several months later God blessed and encouraged us when a young woman believed and became the first faithful member of Cypress Christian Church. The "church" met in our rented house, seated in a circle in the sitting room, enjoying intimate warm fellowship as we worshiped the Lord together.

Sometime later a young elementary school teacher, Mr. Numata, joined our group because he wanted to study English and was somewhat interested in reading the Bible. It wasn't long before Mr. Numata caught me totally off guard by saying that he wanted to be baptized. It was true, he had been attending regularly and listening attentively. (People often said they had to listen carefully to figure out what I was saying, due to my poor language ability.) However, I was surprised by his request because I had come to expect that it would take a long time for Japanese people to come to faith. I asked him why he wanted to be baptized. He replied that he believed in Jesus. I asked him why he had believed in Jesus. He replied that it was because I had told him that Jesus was the only true God. Then he added, "…and because the Bible says so."

I felt relieved and amazed that this man had truly come to faith. We had been praying for his salvation but did not expect him to believe so soon. *Lord, I do believe: help me overcome my unbelief.* After a time of baptismal preparation, Mr. Numata was baptized in the local public bath before the regular business hours commenced. The bath house manager was both surprised and amused to see two people enter the bath fully clothed in freshly laundered baptismal gowns. Normally no clothes are allowed to be worn in a Japanese public bath. The other guests stood around and witnessed Mr. Numata's baptism with great joy.

We first contacted Mrs. Izumi through teaching western cooking classes. She was interested to see how westerners lived in Japan. Sometime later when she expressed interest in hearing a message from the Bible, we invited her to come to church. However, she only attended very infrequently, claiming she couldn't get up in time. She did have a demanding job, going from house to house to collect insurance premiums. We said we would pray that she could wake up in time to come to church. She told her husband what we said and they both laughed.

The following Sunday Mrs. Izumi came in time for church! She told us that she woke up early that morning by sneezing seven times, even though she didn't have a cold or suffer from allergies. However, Mrs. Izumi soon slipped back into her old ways of skipping church on Sundays and we didn't see her for a long time. As the church continued to grow, we were able to rent a house with a single missionary lady living upstairs, while the main floor was used for Cypress Christian Church meetings.

One Sunday morning as I stood up to preach, the door opened. I waited for the person to enter. All eyes turned to see who our late visitor might be. There stood Mrs. Izumi! She suddenly looked startled and hesitant but she came in and sat down. As I was preaching I noticed that Mrs. Izumi could not hold back her tears. She continued to dab her eyes throughout the rest of the service. While people were drinking tea after the service, I sat down next to her and asked how I could pray for her. It seemed to me that God's Word had touched her heart.

When I gently inquired if that was the case, she shook her head. Instead she told me that she had no intention of coming to church that morning. While doing her rounds to collect insurance premiums, she walked through a children's park. The next thing she realized was that she was inside the church building and opening the door, but she didn't know how she got there. Her heart was moved to think that God cared so much for her that He would do such a thing! She sat there crying tears of gratitude to God and tears of remorse for her own resistance.

I wish I could tell you that Mrs. Izumi was consistent in attending church thereafter, but she wasn't. However, we learned from our successors that she eventually came to faith and was baptized.

Mrs. Noto, one of the new believers at Cypress Christian Church, was a young wife. One day when we came home she was waiting at our front door, upset and crying. She and her husband had had an argument. They had been trying for a couple of years to start a family. Finally her doctor suggested she take fertility pills to increase her chances of conceiving, but her husband was adamant that she not take such drugs. She had come to ask for prayer and advice.

She asked if it would be okay to try the fertility pills without telling her husband, as there seemed to be no other way to start a family. We looked at Scripture together and she could see that to deceive her husband was not an option. As he was adamant that she not take the drugs, the only recourse she had was to pray. So we prayed that the Lord would work in her husband's heart, and that they would be able to discuss things amicably. With not much faith, we also prayed that the Lord would give them a child another way.

Three months later Mrs. Noto came to tell us that she was pregnant. God had honored her obedience to His Word and had worked a miracle despite our hesitant faith.

God is always at work in unexpected ways. Through many and varied experiences God was teaching us to ask Him in faith for even greater things than we could imagine.

What do you need to ask God for – something greater than you can imagine? Ask Him! He delights to surprise His children.

4. SQUARE PEGS
IN ROUND HOLES

Pat

*I have become all things to all people so
that by all possible means I might save some.*
- 1 Corinthians 9:22

It is said that you shouldn't put a square peg in a round hole, but sometimes that is the only peg available. That is how I, Pat, felt about teaching cooking classes. Cooking classes in Japan were a wonderful way to reach out to women. Adorned in their pretty aprons, everyone enjoyed the fun of making a tasty meal or cake together and chatting away on a subject of common interest. While the food was in the oven or simmering on the stove, there was a natural time to sing a praise song and hear a short Bible message or testimony. By that time most people felt at home and were quite open to listening. Many Japanese Christian women will confirm that their first contact with the Gospel came through cooking classes.

I had come to Japan when I was 25 and most of what I cooked had been taught to me by Japanese ladies. However, missionaries were expected to hold cooking classes. I felt like a square peg being pushed into the round hole of teaching cooking classes as a means of evangelism. Many Japanese-led churches also liked to ask missionaries to hold an International cooking class as an outreach event, so for that reason too I was in demand for something that was not my gift. There was no way out for me!

One fall, when pumpkins are in abundance, I was invited to do a cooking class at a small Japanese-led church on the south side of Sapporo. I thought it would be a good idea to do something with pumpkins. I decided on a menu of South African pumpkin fritters and German pumpkin cake, a recipe from a German missionary friend.

Twenty-two ladies came. More than half of them were non-believers who had received an invitation to the class. The church ladies were delighted to have this opportunity to invite their friends and to welcome the newcomers.

I was a bit nervous, but set to with the authority of a cooking class instructor. All went well until the heat of the oven in which the cake was rising nicely and the heat of the oil in which we were frying the fritters set off the fire alarm. No one knew how to switch it off. Panic ensued. The continuous screech of the fire alarm did nothing to calm my now-shattered nerves. In the general chaos of flapping aprons, opening windows and shouting instructions to each other, we forgot about the cake. By the time someone finally found out how to shut off the alarm, the cake had burned.

Fortunately we had an extra pumpkin, so we started all over again. While the second cake baked, there was a wonderfully supportive atmosphere as I shared a short Bible message. Somehow I felt that through the chaos, God had set the scene in a very special way to make their hearts receptive to His Word. Afterwards we all enjoyed cinnamon-laced pumpkin fritters and a slice of German pumpkin cake topped with "non-fattening" cream!

~~~~~~~~~~~~~

Another time I was asked to teach "delicious liver" to a group of ladies in a church about 45 minutes from our home. Our three children had to study English for 30 minutes each morning before leaving for their local Japanese school, so time in the mornings was at a premium. Preparation the night before was key. Everything I would need to make "delicious liver" was placed in bags and containers and put at the front door ready to go. Everything that is, except the liver, which had to be kept in the fridge overnight.

The next morning, with the children safely off to school, I packed the bags into the car and went off to my assignment. About halfway there I remembered that the liver was still in the fridge! Not knowing what to do, I parked the car and started crying. Then I found a public phone and called Tony. He suggested I try to buy some liver at a nearby supermarket. He reminded me that God was with me and would help me. The class was supposed to start at 10:00. Supermarkets opened at 10:30 or 11:00, besides which, not all supermarkets carried beef liver. I needed 900 grams.

When I arrived at the supermarket, it was closed. I knocked loudly and the owner came to the door to ask what I wanted. It wasn't every day that he had a frantic foreigner knocking on his door before opening time! I explained that I needed 900 grams of beef liver. He said that the new delivery would not come in before 11:00 but he might have some left over from the day before. He came back smiling and said, "I have just 900 grams left!"

Why did I doubt God? He never said anything about being careful not to put square pegs in round holes. He only said that He will help us and provide all we need to do what He asks of us. I have learned that God cares about His work and His workers. He is always a step ahead in every situation.

Do you feel like a square peg in a round hole? Be assured that God will use you right there!

5. DOES GOD REALLY SPEAK?

Tony

They will call on my name and I will answer them; I will say,
'They are my people,' and they will say, "The Lord is our God."
- Zechariah 13:9

Every Christian parent wants their children to follow the Lord. Our deepest desire for them is that they would know and follow Jesus during their life on earth and be with Him in heaven for eternity. Even before our children were born, Pat and I prayed that they would come to know Jesus and experience the incomparable joy of being loved by Him. God blessed us with three children. Brad and Karen were born in Sapporo, Japan, and Greg in Cape Town, South Africa. It was almost impossible for us to imagine that God's love surpassed our love for them. However, when they tested our patience to the extreme, we could more easily acknowledge that fact, and were thankful that God's love was indeed greater than ours!

One day when I was putting our four-year-old daughter to bed, she asked me, "Daddy, does God really speak?"

"Yes, He does," I replied, thinking that as she grew up and read the Bible, she too would hear God's voice through His written Word.

"But He hasn't spoken to me yet," she said.

"Well, just ask Him," I said. After praying with her, I switched off the light and went downstairs to my wife, who had been working hard in the kitchen.

Early the next morning, her face shining with excitement and joy, my little girl told me that God had spoken to her.

"What did He say?" I asked, half thinking it was probably just her imagination.

"He said, 'Karen, I love you,'" she replied.

"That's lovely," I said, happy that my daughter was so excited to think that God had spoken to her. I went to get something in my bedroom, and that was when I heard God speak to *me*. Everything became quiet. I felt His presence. The voices downstairs faded away, as did other distractions of traffic noise and people talking outside.

I was standing next to my bed when in my spirit a voice spoke. "So you think I did not speak to Karen?" I knew it was the Lord. Then He asked me another question. "What do you think I would say to Karen?"

"I think you would probably say, 'I love you'" I replied.

"Exactly!" God said. The quietness passed and again I became conscious of the children's voices as they played downstairs.

I called my daughter upstairs. Now I was all ears to hear what God had said to her. Without hesitation and with absolute certainty she told me, "God said, 'Karen, I love you.'" I nodded, knowing that God had indeed spoken to her. God had gently but firmly rebuked me for thinking that He would not answer a little girl's prayer of faith. I thought of Jesus' words, "Truly I tell you, unless you change and become like little children, you will never enter the kingdom of heaven" (Matthew 18:3). We should more frequently come to God as little children, full of pure, simple faith, expecting Him to speak to us.

There are many accounts in Scripture of God speaking to people in an audible voice – Moses on the mountain, Abraham under the great trees at Mamre, Isaiah in his vision of God in the temple, Samuel as a boy serving under Eli the priest, and Saul on his way to Damascus, to name only a few. Most of us do not have that kind of experience, yet we know when God has spoken to us.

Dennis, a friend in Cape Town who worked for Youth for Christ, was a mentor to Pat and me in preparing us to go to Japan as missionaries. One day Dennis related this incident. He had witnessed to a neighbor who lived a few streets away. Late one night Dennis sensed that God was telling him to visit that neighbor. Initially he dismissed the thought, as it was after eleven o'clock. *How can you just pop in to visit someone at this hour?* He reasoned. But the voice in his spirit persisted. Reluctantly he obeyed.

The house appeared to be in darkness and Dennis resolved to return home and go to bed. However, the sense that God was telling him to visit persisted, so he walked around to the back of the house. To his surprise, the kitchen light was on. When he gently knocked on the door, a disheveled neighbor welcomed him in. He was in a desperate situation and contemplating suicide.

Over a period of time Dennis was able to counsel this neighbor and lead him to Christ. The man became good friends with both Dennis and the Lord. Dennis' story taught me that we must obey when God speaks, even when His prompting seems unreasonable.

Another instance of hearing God speak occurred during a family vacation at Takayama by the sea, near Sendai City in Japan. Every summer missionaries rented several of the wooden beach houses that were more than one hundred years old. We looked forward to a much-needed rest and unhurried times of fellowship. Chapel services were held on Sundays.

One summer several of us (then) young missionaries sat on the beach discussing who might be the next Superintendent of OMF's work in Japan. The Superintendent cared for and supervised the missionaries. We tossed around various names as we considered possible candidates. Not surprisingly, none of us lazing in the summer sun made the list!

That same summer a guest speaker from America with a pronounced southern accent spoke in a chapel service. I don't remember much of the message except that he repeated many times, "God said: 'Will ya or won't ya?'" (By interpretation – will you or won't you obey what I am telling you to do?) I could not imagine God speaking that way. However, the words "Will ya or won't ya?" began to play like a recording in my head.

After vacation we all returned to our places of ministry. No announcement of the name of the new Superintendent was forthcoming. At that time Pat and I were involved in a church plant on the northwest side of Sapporo. An enthusiastic young German couple had joined us and we were glad to be part of a team.

One evening as I returned from teaching an outreach English class, I noticed the OMF Director's car parked outside our house. I wondered why he was there. My wife and I were in for a shock! As we drank tea together, the Director asked me to consider taking on the Superintendent role. We started to name people we thought would be more suitable, but he just shook his head. After more discussion, we agreed to pray about his proposal. The Director drove off and we were left staring at each other, questions racing through our minds.

Our children were happily settled in the local Japanese school and kindergarten. The Sunday school was well attended with more than twenty children – mostly friends of our three children. Our new team members had only been with us for about a year. Would they be expected to take on the leadership of the church alone? If we accepted, could we perhaps divide our time between the Superintendent role and the church? This proposal was flatly rejected by our Japan Field Council on the grounds that it would be too much work. Secondly, if we continued at the church, leadership would not fully transition to the younger missionary couple, gifted and able as they both were.

The appointment would mean a complete upheaval for our family with a move to another area of Sapporo closer to the OMF office. Our heads were in turmoil. Our children vigorously resisted the thought of leaving their schools and their friends. *Why did this proposal come at this inopportune time?*

Then I heard those words again in my head, "Will ya or won't ya?" Was this really God speaking? Would He speak to me like *that*? Somehow I knew it was God. During that summer vacation He had prepared my heart to be the next Superintendent.

When God calls, the whole family is included. It was a difficult decision for us as parents. However, our children soon made friends at their new schools. Maybe that was partially because they were fluent in Japanese, but also no doubt because of God's special care for our children.

The new missionaries did an excellent job, and the church continued to grow. To this day it stands as a beacon to the people in that area, proclaiming that God's voice can be heard if you are willing to listen.

Have you heard God speaking to you? It may come through a child. It may come in unexpected ways. It may even seem unreasonable. But if you listen carefully, you will hear Him speak. And He will never ask something of us without giving us the resources needed to accomplish the task. The best way to hear His voice is to read the Bible every day. As you obey His Word and become familiar with His ways, you will hear Him speak ever so much more clearly and assuredly.

Yes, God really does speak to us.

6. A NEW TOOL IN MY BAG

Pat

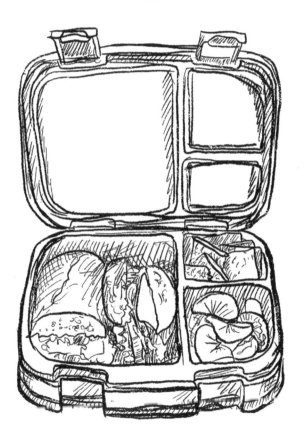

*Therefore, since we are surrounded by such a great cloud of
witnesses, let us throw off everything that hinders,
and the sin that so easily entangles. And let us
run with perseverance the race marked out for us.*
- Hebrews 12:1

In 1990 the Lord opened the door for us to immigrate to Canada, as South Africans were no longer being given visas to Japan. Although we were amazed at how the Lord had guided and how He had so wonderfully opened the door for us to come to Canada, arriving as new immigrants with three teenagers who were pining for Japan was not easy.

Saying goodbye to family and friends in our beloved South Africa, not knowing if we would ever be able to afford to return, seemed a harder decision than when we first left South Africa to go to Japan as missionaries 20 years before. Arriving in Vancouver I, Pat, felt as if I had lost my moorings. I now belonged to a country, to a city about which I knew nothing. I was grieving not only the loss of my dear friends in Japan, but also the loss of my homeland, South Africa.

Every day I barely managed to make the lunches for the children and send them off to school, before flopping down on the bed and crying. This pattern went on for about three months. My sense of lostness only increased as the children started making arrangements to meet friends in places I had never heard of. Were they safe? Did they know how to discern who were good friends and who weren't? I felt that I was "losing it," but didn't know how to turn around.

Our home in Vancouver was also the OMF Mission Home, and one day a fellow missionary came to stay. She gave me an article about a woman who had lost her husband and how she had dealt with her grief. As I read the article through my tears I said, "Lord, she only lost her husband, but I have lost all my friends in Japan and also all my family and friends in South Africa and even South Africa as my homeland!" As I said these words aloud to God, it was as if I came to my senses. I thought, *I have truly gone over the edge. Losing a husband is far worse than all the things I listed. I can't even think straight anymore!* I was afraid of what was becoming of me.

The next day I went to church with a renewed sense that I needed to listen to what God might be saying to me. In a sudden change of plans, the pastor asked a lady visitor to give her testimony instead of him preaching his message. She spoke on Hebrews 12:1. Then she looked at us (at *me?*) and said, "Is there any sin in your life that is entangling you so that you cannot run the race?" I responded to the Lord as honestly as I knew how. I said, "Lord, I don't think my problem is sin. I'm not really doing anything. All I'm doing is crying."

And then it came, the Lord's clear voice in my heart. "Pat, beware of self-pity. Self-pity is a sin." I was astounded. Was that my problem? It must be, if the Lord said so. I asked the Lord what I should do. And He said, "Stop crying."

The next morning after the children went off to school came the biggest test of all. I so badly wanted to just flop on the bed and cry. But God had spoken, and I knew I couldn't do that anymore.

I struggled for a few days and then, like a mist that evaporates, the heavy depression and sadness left me. From then on when I received a letter from friends in Japan, I could smile and rejoice.

They were where God had put them and I was here, where God had put me. It all seemed so right. God had set me free to once again fulfill His purposes for me.

Self-pity is an insidious sin that can rob us of perspective. We become blinded to what God is doing or might want to do through us. We become wrapped up in self instead of being content with what God has given. We lose our generous spirit and find that we cannot love God or people as we should.

I knew that God had given me a new tool in my bag – the ability to view things from His perspective. Do you need that tool too?

7. THE AURORA TEAM

Tony

*Let your light shine before people, that they may see your good
deeds and praise your Father in heaven.*
- Matthew 5:16

Whatever could have possessed us to take fourteen
elementary school children on a two-week short-term mission
trip to Japan? It began one Sunday while we were sitting in the
service of our home church in Vancouver and thinking, *Lord,
how can we make the needs of Japan known to our church family? They
are so involved in their local programs.* The thought came, *Take their
children to Japan, and they will get interested.*

Was it God? We believed it was. Fourteen children applied
and all were accepted. They ranged in age from 10 to 12. The
only criterion was that they should have a faith in Jesus which
they wanted to share with others. We knew there would be some
rough times during our time in Japan, and we needed to be sure
we could appeal to their faith in Jesus to help them persevere.
The church choir leader and the youth pastor joined Pat and me
as the adult leaders.

The group chose the name Aurora, possibly because of some
of the colorful characters on the team, or perhaps because it was
an appropriate name to represent Canada. The Aurora Borealis,
also called the Northern Lights, originate in the polar region.
Many visitors come to Canada every year to view the magnificent
displays of green, red and yellow lights moving across the night
sky. It was also our sincere prayer that the team would be the
light of Jesus to the places we would be visiting while in Japan.

The Aurora Team met often to prepare. They learned some simple Japanese phrases such as greetings, please, thank you, simple self-introductions, and where is the washroom? It was a lot of fun as we bonded together and practised hard to perfect the programs we planned to present. The children even learned to sing some Japanese choruses.

To raise the two thousand dollars that each child needed, the Aurora Team washed vehicles, baked cookies, served meals at the church, and even 'kidnapped' some people, including the pastor, whose families had to pay a voluntary ransom of any amount for their release. The whole church got involved and started to develop a genuine mission interest in Japan.

Arrangements were made with five churches in Japan for the team to sing, share a short testimony, play games with children, and visit a local school where they would take part in the day's program. For me, it would be mainly preaching a sermon in Japanese in four of the churches. Homestay accommodations were arranged with families of children who attended the churches or local schools. Japanese Bibles and some Canadian mementos were given to each homestay family as a thank you gift.

The homestays initially proved to be a steep learning curve for the Aurora Team and for the two assistant managers.

One of the biggest challenges for the children was Japanese food. Most children do not have a sense of adventure when it comes to food. Some children were so excited when their host said they would have taco for supper. They thought they would be having Mexican tacos but instead they were given raw octopus, which is *tako* in Japanese. One hostess asked Pat the following morning, "Is it true that Canadian children have cake and Coca Cola for breakfast?" She noticed the two children staying with her didn't eat much breakfast, so she asked them, "What do you have for breakfast in Canada?" The children must have replied "cake and Coca Cola"! We had to have a few serious talks with the children!

The foreign children from Canada were a big hit wherever they went. Japanese people love children and welcomed ours warmly. At the first church we visited, the pastor and members doubted whether there would be more Japanese children than Aurora kids coming to the meeting they had advertised. Their children's ministry was almost non-existent at the time. Imagine their surprise when 120 children showed up, perhaps mostly because of our prior visit to their local school.

The day we visited the local Japanese school was memorable. We were able to take the team to the school in Sapporo where our own children had attended. The team was invited to participate in some classes with the Japanese children. The entire school turned out to welcome us as we walked up the hill to the school gates. The brass band was playing, people were clapping and cheering and shouting greetings to us, and a TV camera crew was there to record the event. We felt like Olympic gold medalists!

Introductions and good wishes were exchanged. One of the classes they participated in was a Japanese brush writing class. With the TV cameras in the classroom, the teacher became so nervous that he made a mistake in writing the character on the blackboard for the children to copy. The local children were giggling, but would not correct their teacher as it would have appeared rude. I noticed that the cameraman did not point the camera at the blackboard in a face-saving act of kindness. The only students who copied the character with the teacher's mistake were the Aurora Team. The Japanese children all quietly wrote the character correctly on their pages.

All the children ate the usual lunch (*kyuushoku*) provided by the school. They really enjoyed the delicious food and creamy Hokkaido milk.

As I watched the happy faces of the children enjoying each other's company despite the language barrier, I thought about the words of Psalm 133:1, "How good and pleasant it is when brothers (and sisters) live together in unity!" All the teachers were smiling, relieved to see the children enjoying themselves so much. They must have been under a lot of stress beforehand, wondering how it would all turn out.

Although we were not able to openly evangelize in the school, we were introduced on the TV recording as coming from a church in Canada. As it turned out, it was good PR for the local church, since many of the children came to an event held later at the church. At the end of the school day the children were sad to say goodbye to each other. God had indeed blessed us all with wonderful, happy memories of that day.

Another day we visited a Japanese couple who were our friends. We invited our youth pastor to join us, just to give him another experience. He could not speak any Japanese, so from time to time we interpreted for him. At one point he asked if he could use the washroom. The toilet was computerized and could be operated manually or by selecting one of the functions on a panel. Needless to say, the functions of the buttons were written only in Japanese.

After what seemed a long time, the youth pastor rejoined us in the sitting room, looking a bit flustered. On the way home he told us what had happened. He was sitting on the toilet when curiosity got the better of him. He began to experiment by pressing a few buttons. Suddenly a fountain of water spurted up directly under him. The problem was that he didn't know which button to press to stop the fountain. All he could do was to try a few more buttons. The temperature of the water alternated between hot and cold, strong stream and gentle. What could he do but pray? After a time he must have hit the right button to stop the water. I think he learned the lesson: When in doubt – don't!

On a free day we all took a trip to the wonderful department stores. It had started to rain as we left so we each took an umbrella. After a time the rain stopped so the adults became the baggage carriers for the children's umbrellas. They were sure to misplace them as they excitedly looked at all the interesting items for sale. Although we had divided the children into four groups with an adult leader responsible for each group, I was constantly looking over my shoulder as we went up the escalators, counting heads to make sure there were still eighteen people in our party. It was exhausting! At the end of our shopping spree we were relieved to have everyone safely back in their various homestays.

In one of the cities where our team ministered, the local missionary arranged for an outing on our day off. Pat was instructed to follow the missionary who had some of the children in his van. She had four children in her little car as she followed him through the city. At one point she saw his van change into the right lane. There was a bus stopped on Pat's left, but she was looking to see where the van was going to keep following it and didn't notice a child darting out in front of the bus to cross the street. In that split second, Pat knew she could not avoid hitting the little girl. But then she saw her on the sidewalk on the other side of the street! She knew that was impossible, and that God had surely sent an angel to carry the little girl to safety. Pat's knees turned to jelly as she thought what would have happened if she had hit a child in Japan while visiting from Canada. God in His mercy had saved us from an unthinkable disaster.

Before we left Canada the children learned a graphic way to present the Gospel, which they were able to demonstrate at all our events except the school meeting. Placing a silver coin (representing people) on a saucer (the earth), they poured a black liquid (representing sin) into the saucer to cover the coin (showing how sin separates us from God). Lighting a small candle (Jesus as the Light of the World), they placed it on the saucer to burn. An empty glass (representing God's judgment of sin) was brought down on the candle (Jesus, the Light of the World). When the oxygen in the glass expired, the flame went out (Jesus' death), drawing all the black liquid into the glass and leaving the coin (representing forgiven sinners) clean and dry.

This object lesson dramatically showed how Jesus took our sin on Himself, dying to make us clean and free to have a relationship with God again. Pat and I walked around the tables offering extra explanations in Japanese so that everyone understood the Gospel message. At the end, some of the local people were doing the demonstration, explaining the meaning of the Gospel to each other. Praise God! One lady, whose husband had not believed yet, was visibly moved. She said, "The demonstration was so powerful and understandable. I am going home now to explain to my husband what Jesus has done for me." We prayed that his heart would be open.

Towards the end of the two weeks some of the younger children started to get a bit homesick, but the older children encouraged the younger ones to persevere for Jesus' sake. Finally we boarded the plane to fly back to Vancouver. Everyone was soon fast asleep, happily tired after all their excitement and different experiences. Not only did we have wonderful ministry opportunities, but we were also blessed by the love and kindness of many Japanese people. As we journeyed home we prayed that God would continue to use the light cast by the Aurora Team to penetrate the spiritual darkness so prevalent in Japan.

Upon our arrival at Vancouver Airport there was an emotional crowd of parents and friends to welcome us back. We noticed that it was not only the children who were crying!

Pat and I came home thanking the Lord for keeping us all safe, and for the many blessings we had received. God had used the Aurora Team to shine His love and light into many hearts. We gratefully climbed into our bed and woke up nearly twenty hours later! We hadn't realized how tired we were.

You may not be a member of a team called Aurora but if you are a believer, Jesus says you are the light of the world (Matthew 5:14). Keep on shining for Him!

8. WEEPING AND REJOICING

Tony

He who goes out weeping carrying seed to sow,
will return with songs of joy.
- Psalm 126:6 (ESV)

My heart felt heavy as I heard our oldest son sigh deeply as he walked past me in our home in the city of Richmond in Metro Vancouver, Canada. He was missing his friends in Japan. We had accepted God's guidance to emigrate from South Africa to Canada in order to be able to return to Japan as missionaries, because South Africans were no longer being given visas to Japan. Pat and I planned to return to Japan after our children had finished their higher education.

All three children were struggling to find their place in their new country, but it was hardest for our oldest son, who arrived in Canada at the beginning of his grade 12 year. As soon as we spoke, people asked us, "Where do you come from?" Our accent betrayed our non-Canadian roots. But by God's grace, we all managed to find our feet in our new country, which now feels like home.

About five years into our stay in Vancouver, we started to prepare to return to Japan. In order to make sure that our move was according to God's timing, we prayerfully decided to trust the Lord to fulfill what we saw as three conditions that had to be met before we could leave.

First, we needed a replacement for my role as Regional Director for OMF in the province of British Columbia. We felt it would not be right to move back to Japan and leave the position unfilled.

Secondly, the Mission required us to have 100% prayer and financial support to enable us to return. This seemed an impossible target, as our financial support had dropped to about 35% since we had left South Africa to immigrate to Canada.

Thirdly, we wanted our children to understand and support our desire to return as being God's plan for the family. Although they would be staying in Canada while Pat and I went to Japan, we desired their blessing and agreement.

It was a faith-stretching time for all of us as we prayed for nearly two years for God to grant these three requests.

In His good time, God supplied a very experienced couple to fill the Regional Director role. They had returned to Canada from a stressful and dangerous situation in the country where they had been serving as missionaries.

Amazingly, by the time we left for Japan to resume church planting work, our financial support had risen to 100% for the first time in our missionary career.

Hudson Taylor, founder of the China Inland Mission, now known as OMF International, said, "In any work of God there are three stages – impossible, difficult, and done." These words resonated deeply in our hearts as we saw the Lord supply our needs. The God of the impossible always accomplishes that which He purposes to do.

Although it was difficult, our children all agreed that God had called us to go back to Japan, so in theory they approved! Of course the practice was much harder than the theory.

As we prepared to leave for Japan, our final words to our children were that they must love and support each other, because there would be times of stress and difficulty ahead. It reminded us of Jesus' words to His disciples before He left to return to the Father: "As I have loved you, love one another." We had mixed emotions. The joy of God's supply and His affirmation that the time had come for us to return to Japan was contrasted with the sadness of leaving our three children behind in Canada. By then, Brad was recently employed and Greg and Karen were studying at Bible College and University.

At a farewell service of a supporting Chinese church in Vancouver, we gave a testimony thanking them for their love and support. As we sang the hymn "How Great Thou Art," I felt a lump in my throat as I sang the words:

> And when I think that God, His Son not sparing,
> Sent Him to die, I scarce can take it in,
> That on the cross, my burden gladly bearing,
> He bled and died to take away my sin.

I was greatly comforted by the thought that the Father Himself had experienced the same kind of sorrow, yet to a much greater degree than we were feeling. He could absolutely identify with us. It came as a fresh blessing to us to know that we were privileged to share, in a very small way, something of the pain that God the Father must have felt in sending His only Son, Jesus, to earth. The Father had to turn his back on His Son as He suffered on the cross for our sins. Jesus, who had no sin, took on the guilt and shame of our sin, bearing the punishment due to us. The pain of our pending separation from our children could not be compared to the Father's!

At the end of the service we knelt on the stage while the pastor and elders placed their hands on us and prayed. We were overwhelmed by their love and kindness and went home renewed in the knowledge that God takes care of His own. Our children would be in His good hands.

When we arrived back in Japan, the Mission proposed that we do church planting work in either Tokyo or Hokkaido. We had spent all our previous years in Hokkaido and felt more familiar doing evangelism there than in the huge metropolis of Tokyo. While doing a three-month language refresher course in Sapporo, Hokkaido, one small church we visited was celebrating their Christmas event in the local neighborhood hall. The few members were rushing around preparing for the program to begin. As we worked alongside them, setting up tables, chairs, plates and chopsticks, we felt a great love for this small group of believers, and a desire welled up within us to add our prayers and energy to establish a church with them in that location. And so began a wonderful, blessed ten years with a growing group of believers whose love and kindness often overwhelmed us.

One of the believers allowed the church to rent a house that she and her husband owned in the neighborhood. It was a very suitable house with space for parking in the front. However, as the number of believers increased, we had to look for a larger building. It was a good problem to have.

Although we all searched the area diligently, we could not find anything suitable to rent. Buying land and a building was way beyond our capacity, so we kept praying and looking. "Lord, we need a bigger place to welcome new people," we prayed.

One day a believer excitedly reported that a building that had been used as a *juku* near the church-house had just been advertised for sale. A *juku* is a cram school where students receive extra teaching after school hours. The *juku* needed to move to larger premises. The building was located near a bus stop and, upon inspection, appeared to be in excellent condition. We were filled with excitement and anticipation as we thought of the added space we would enjoy. The only problem would be finding the money to buy the land and building, as we had discovered it was not available for rent. Our small group of believers prayed earnestly for the Lord's guidance and provision.

Pat and I had been teaching English as an outreach for the church and that income could be applied towards the purchase of a building. Even then, together with gifts and loans from the church members and ECA (now JECA – Japan Evangelical Church Association) and an advanced loan from the Mission, we were still far short of the asking price.

We decided to prayerfully make an offer even though, humanly speaking, it was too low to be taken seriously. To our great surprise, the bid was accepted a few days later by the owners of the *juku*! We were amazed and thankful to the Lord for His provision.

The building was tastefully renovated for use as a church, with seating room for 70 people. With much fun and excitement the believers decided on colors for the chairs, carpets and curtains, and the type of characters for writing the name of the church on the building. Amidst great rejoicing, we held an opening service to dedicate the property to be used for the glory of God.

After that the church enjoyed a time of great blessing. A young lady from the UK joined us as an English teacher, so the number of contacts with local people continued to increase. There was love, joy, peace and growth in the church. Each morning as I unlocked the door I would say, "Bless the Lord, O my soul and all that is within me, bless His holy name!" I felt such joy working there. As believers were trained to lead the expanding number of small groups, numbers increased. They were happy to invite their friends to these smaller, more intimate gatherings. Four people per group served each week in leading a time of fun, praise, Bible study and prayer. When the number of people in a group exceeded eight, we would form another group, and so the numbers continued to grow.

On average, the number of people baptized per year in a Japanese church is two or less. One year we baptized eleven believers. A newcomer attending the church came to me one Sunday a bit confused, saying, "We always have communion on the first Sunday and baptism on the third Sunday, but this month no one is being baptized – why, what's wrong?" Since he had begun attending the church that was the usual order he had witnessed each month. The church grew to such an extent that we had to hold two worship services every Sunday morning. I do not want to give the impression that there were no problems or difficulties. There were, as there are in every church. However, in this church there was far more rejoicing than weeping!

As a follower of Jesus, are you experiencing a time of weeping? May the Lord help you to persevere – a time of rejoicing will come!

"He who goes out weeping carrying seed to sow, will return with songs of joy" (Psalm 126:5-6, ESV).

9. THE TRUTH WILL SET YOU FREE

Pat

Then you will know the truth, and the truth will set you free.
- John 8:32

Many times in Japan we lamented, "Is there no one who is seeking the truth?" There were not many. But there were some...

A lady knocked on the door of the church one day and asked, "Can you please tell me the truth about Jesus Christ?" Mrs. Oka had been studying with the Jehovah's Witnesses who are very active in Japan. It started when a mother of one of the children in her son's class asked Mrs. Oka if she would like to study what the Bible says about bringing up children. She thought that would be helpful, so she started meeting regularly with her. As time went on, her JW friend started talking about Jesus, but somewhere Mrs. Oka had heard that Jesus was actually God. She realized that what her friend was saying was very different. She began to feel uncomfortable, but she knew that to stop the studies would hurt their friendship. She had seen that there was a little church just down the road from her home, so she decided to ask there concerning the truth about Jesus.

"What is the truth about Jesus Christ?" This is the question that every Christian missionary who comes to Japan longs to answer! The missionary who answered the door that day welcomed Mrs. Oka in and encouraged her to study the Christian Bible with her. That was the beginning.

It took a few years of study and interaction with Japanese Christians as well before Mrs. Oka finally accepted Jesus Christ as her Lord and Savior. Once she decided to get baptized, she experienced the freedom that Jesus promised. She felt free to tell her JW friend about her new-found faith and the truth about Jesus Christ that she had come to understand and believe.

She came to know the truth, and the truth had set her free!

~~~~~~~~~~~~

In another church, one of the Christians, Mrs. Abe, told us her story. She had been studying with the Jehovah's Witnesses for five years. Then she met a Christian missionary whose child was in the same elementary school class as her daughter. They chatted and shared backgrounds. When the missionary asked her if she had a Bible, she said she was studying with the Jehovah's Witnesses. The missionary asked, "Have you received a blessing from those studies?" It was God's voice to Mrs. Abe. The question kept troubling her, because she realized that she had never felt blessed by their studies. *I've studied for five years and have not received any blessing,* she thought, *so why am I continuing?* The missionary came to visit her a few days later and brought her a Bible, but Mrs. Abe couldn't pluck up the courage to take it. She had been well indoctrinated. Jehovah's Witnesses are not permitted to read the Christian Bible.

However, that question—"Have you received a blessing from those studies?"—kept ringing in her ears. Finally Mrs. Abe decided to stop the studies with the Jehovah's Witnesses, and asked the missionary for a Christian Bible.

As Mrs. Abe read and studied with the missionary, she met Jesus, Son of God, in the pages of the Bible. The joy of her discovery bubbled up within her, and she knew that this was the blessing she had been seeking. She had found her Savior – the One who promises eternal life and forgiveness of sins to all who believe.

When we came to take over the leadership of the church

where she was a member, Mrs. Abe had grown as a Christian and was already a pillar in the little church, and actively serving as a faithful witness in her neighborhood.

She came to know the truth, and the truth had set her free.

~~~~~~~~~~~~~~

In the first church where we served in Sapporo, on a lovely summer day we were having an outdoor worship service. We noticed a couple with two little boys edging nearer to our group as if they wanted to listen. We invited them to join us. Mr. and Mrs. Maruyama seemed so happy to be with us, and enjoyed the fellowship afterwards, forgoing their own plans for a family picnic. One of the believers invited them to church the next Sunday, but they said they were already studying the Bible with the Jehovah's Witnesses.

As this was the first church plant we were leading and our language wasn't up to much, we asked the senior Japanese member of our small group to try to persuade them to stop studying with the JWs and come to the church for Bible study. We suggested he tell them the truth that the JWs were a relatively recent religion formed in the USA and not part of traditional Christianity.

Our brother shook his head and said he couldn't do that. It would be infringing on their privacy, and they would never respect him again if he did that. We didn't yet have a feel for the Japanese culture and were dismayed by his decision. Surely we wouldn't let them be led astray when there was a chance to bring the truth of the wonderful Gospel of Jesus Christ to them! Finally our brother conceded, "OK, you talk to them. You are foreigners. They won't expect you to understand Japanese etiquette." So we did.

However, Mr. and Mrs. Maruyama said they could not stop studying with the JWs, as that would be rude. We boldly assured them that they could leave the JWs to us. "Just give us their phone number and we will politely tell them that you are now studying with us," we told them. Maybe because they didn't know how to handle such persuasive foreigners, they gave us the phone number and promised to come to church the next Sunday.

The long saga that followed with the JWs tested not only our Japanese language skills, but also our faith. Did we only believe that Jesus was truly God because we had been brought up that way? Did we believe only because we had been taught that way? We decided to read the whole New Testament again with new and inquiring eyes. What a blessing! There is no doubt at all. There is no way you could read the New Testament and not come to the absolute conviction that Jesus Christ is the Messiah, the Son of the Living God. In fact He is the One to whom the whole Old Testament points.

Mr. and Mrs. Maruyama and their two little boys came to church every Sunday after that. In our studies with them it was a joy to introduce them to the Triune God—Father, Son and Holy Spirit. It took a while, but eventually the Maruyamas believed and were baptized.

They came to know the truth, and the truth had set them free!

It is a tragedy that in Japan where there are so few Christians (less than 1%), many false religions, often claiming to be Christian, are eagerly working to draw people in. If you have been set free by the truth of Jesus Christ, will you join us in praying to the Lord of the Harvest to send many more workers to Japan to proclaim the One who is The Truth?

Maybe He will send you! You would be welcome indeed!

10. DRAWN TO THE LIGHT

Pat

I have come into the world as a light, so that no one who
believes in me should stay in darkness.
- John 12:46

Imagine the trauma of a three-year-old girl who is taken from her mother and father and given to an aunt who has no children. This, however, was quite a common practice in Japan several decades ago. Mikiko, who had come from a family of five children, suddenly became the only child of a busy, hard-working farmer couple. She remembers always feeling unloved and sad and terribly, terribly lonely. When she was about 10 years old she heard for the first time that she was adopted. She heard her "cousins" say that their mother, her birth mother, had died. Her sense of not belonging only increased as she seemed unable to meet the expectations of her aunt and uncle, who felt she did not do farm work well. She was scolded constantly, and the loneliness and darkness in her heart often overwhelmed her.

She never knew why it was there, but hanging on the wall of the room where she slept was a picture entitled "The Infant Samuel at Prayer" by Sir Joshua Reynolds. To her, it was a picture of a little girl praying towards a light. She identified with that "little girl" and felt strangely comforted and drawn to that light as she often cried herself to sleep at night. *Someday,* she thought, *I will find that light.*

Mikiko grew up, married, and had two sons of her own. At one point the family moved to Sapporo, the main city on the northern island of Hokkaido. Mikiko loved to cook. One day she received an invitation in her letter box to attend an international cooking class. She immediately applied. She ran a small boarding house for students and enjoyed trying the new recipes on her family and boarders. The cooking classes were hosted by missionaries who had moved into her area, as a way of reaching out to the local women.

At each cooking class, while the prepared dish was baking in the oven or cooking on the stove, the ladies sat around tables and listened to a short message from the Bible given by the missionary. Sometimes they heard a testimony from a Japanese Christian.

At first Mikiko listened without much interest, but as time went by she realized that she was being challenged to believe these messages, not just listen to them. She struggled to sort it out in her mind. She was, after all, a Buddhist. She had always been a Buddhist and all her family were Buddhists. Why should she believe in this Jesus Christ?

One day a thought came to her. *Buddha was a great teacher. Jesus Christ was a great teacher. But Buddha is dead, and Jesus Christ is still alive.* "Well then," she said to herself, "I will believe in Jesus Christ." That settled it for Mikiko. She had made her decision and went on to be baptized. She was added to the small body of believers in her neighborhood and was always a smiling encouragement to everyone.

Years later, while looking for a gift for her son's wedding, she went to a Christian bookstore in downtown Sapporo. As she was browsing, something caught her eye. It was a small pile of postcards with the picture of "The Infant Samuel at Prayer" by Sir Joshua Reynolds. She was intrigued! She inquired at the desk about who the "little girl" in the picture was, and why that picture was on some postcards in the Christian bookshop. When she heard that it was a picture of Samuel, she was delighted. She knew the story of Samuel from reading her Bible.

She stood and looked deeply at the picture, and the memories of those difficult years on her adoptive parents' farm came flooding back. Tears rolled down her cheeks. But this time they were tears of unbelievable joy! God had seen her even then. God had heard that little girl's plea so many years ago. He had seen her tears, and He had led her to the Light.

She has indeed found the Light – Jesus Christ, the Light of the World!

Have you found that Light?

11. A BRUISED REED

Tony

A bruised reed he will not break,
and a smouldering wick he will not snuff out.
- Isaiah 42:3

Ichiro was desperate to find a way out of his hopeless situation. He thought that the only way to end his intense misery would be to commit suicide by throwing himself in front of a train. From the top of an overpass he could see down the tracks to a station in the distance. He sat down to wait for the next train to come. It wouldn't be long now....

I first met Ichiro and his wife Rika as a young couple who had recently moved into our neighborhood. Pat and I felt an affinity with them from the start, which deepened as we got to know each other better.

Neither Ichiro nor his wife Rika had ever heard the Gospel. This is not surprising in a society where less than half of one percent of the population are Christians. However, as a fourteen-year-old schoolboy walking home from the shrine where he had gone to seek atonement for letting his pet bird die, Ichiro saw a Gideon New Testament at the foot of an idol. He picked it up and took it home. He did not read it much because he found the words difficult to understand. But this was when he first heard of Jesus Christ.

Many years later, after he had married and settled down, Ichiro experienced a long period of extreme busyness, and strained relationships at work. He became increasingly tired and depressed. Totally exhausted, he felt he was a failure because he could not cope with life. Ichiro's wife, Rika, knew that her husband was contemplating suicide, but she didn't know what she could do to help him. Medication had not helped. Nothing seemed to help. Ichiro had reached the point of no return.

And so it was that he sat down near the railway track one day and waited for a train to leave the station. Ichiro waited and waited, but the train remained stationary. As the sun began to set, Ichiro thought about his parents, and decided to go back to his hometown. The next morning he read a report in the local newspaper about a man who had committed suicide the previous afternoon by throwing himself in front of a train. Ichiro suddenly realized that this was the reason 'his train' had not come!

He felt that he had been spared death by someone else taking his place that day. He then recalled reading a book by a well-known Christian author, Ayako Miura. Her book was based on the true account of a young Christian man on board a train climbing up the steep and winding Shiokari Pass in northern Hokkaido. Near the end of the pass where the railway line started to level out, suddenly the last passenger carriage became uncoupled and started to roll backwards. The young man, Masao Nagano, perhaps thought, *I am probably the only person on this train who knows Jesus, and so is sure of eternal life.* In a heroic act of love, he lowered himself from the train onto the tracks. As the wheels ploughed into his body, the carriage ground to a halt, saving the lives of the other passengers from certain death.

This story had made a deep impact on Ichiro as he thought about the courage that young man must have possessed to do something so selfless. *Why did he sacrifice himself?* he wondered. It was then that Ichiro once again began to read the New Testament he had found so many years before.

Around Christmas time one year, Ichiro could not sleep, so he watched TV throughout the night. Early the next morning, he saw a blind lady playing the piano. She seemed so peaceful and sang with such a beautiful voice that his spirit was touched. After she sang, there was a Bible presentation, at which point Ichiro realized that he was watching a Christian program.

As he listened, he felt no animosity towards what was being said, because he was desperately seeking answers to the meaning of life. Was there really a god out there who could help him? Because of the extreme stress he had been experiencing, Ichiro had quit going to work and was just wandering around aimlessly searching for relief. But unknown to him, God was leading him step by step.

On another day he viewed a TV program called *Life Line*. At the end of the presentation the pastor said, "I'll see you next week." The following week's program featured the testimony of Arthur Holland. He rode a cool motorbike, and seemed to Ichiro to be a very unconventional Christian! Arthur shared that he had experienced a turbulent youth, but his heart had been changed when he heard that Jesus had given His life to take the punishment for the sins of someone like him. Ichiro was amazed. *Could it be this Jesus, who gave his life for me?*

Four years into their marriage, Ichiro and Rika moved to the area where we lived. Rika was keen to learn English. On the notice board of a supermarket, she found a flyer advertising English classes which were being held at a neighborhood church. It struck Ichiro that the church's name was one of those listed in the Life Line program, where they recommended that the listeners find "a church near you." He said to Rika, "You go and learn English. I am going to attend the worship service."

I can still clearly recall the first time this young couple came to the church. Sitting near the front, they listened attentively to what was preached from the Word of God. From that time on they were regular attendees every Sunday, and later at small group fellowships too. They were growing in their faith, but the real breakthrough occurred after viewing the movie *The Passion of the Christ*. Ichiro said, "When I watched the movie, I was torn apart by the sight of the Lord Jesus carrying His own cross on His bloodied body after suffering such a cruel whipping. Then I knew for sure that when I was thinking of death, it was this Jesus who had died in my place. I was so moved that I thought my heart would break."

Ichiro and Rika were baptized together. At their baptism they shared from Isaiah 53:5: "But he was pierced for our transgressions, he was crushed for our iniquities; the punishment that brought us peace was upon him, and by his wounds we are healed."

All who witnessed their baptism and heard their testimony were moved by their passion to reach out to others. Just as Jesus saved us, so He wants to save others too. No one is beyond His grace. Though we may feel worthless, God loves us so much that He gave His Son to die for us.

Everyone needs to hear about the passionate love of God and the selfless sacrifice that Jesus made on our behalf.

After Ichiro's baptism, I began to meet with him every Thursday for early morning Bible study and prayer before he went to work. It was a blessed time for both of us as we grew in our knowledge of the Word and in warm fellowship with each other.

Although Ichiro still experienced a lot of stress from long work hours and difficult relationships at his new job, he was beginning to cope better with his problems. The Holy Spirit was at work in his life.

Sometime later Ichiro said, "Since believing in the Lord Jesus, I was able to make many friends, and I have been given a loving wife and daughter. I would like to express my sincere gratitude to the Lord Jesus for dying for me. I'm really glad I didn't die that day at the railway track when I had given up all hope."

Ichiro was a badly bruised reed, but God lovingly and gently rescued and restored him and his wife. They both went on to become leaders in the church, encouraging many on the Road of Faith.

Perhaps you feel that you are a bruised reed or just a smoldering wick. Take heart! Jesus loves you and values you! He wants to strengthen you to fulfill the plans He has for you.

12. CHOICES

Pat

Choose for yourselves this day whom you will serve....
But as for me and my household, we will serve the Lord.
- Joshua 24:15

Omoto-kun became a good friend of our sons, and so his mother and I, Pat, became friends too. Mrs. Omoto and I often chatted with each other. As time went by she also started coming to some of the cooking class outreaches at our little church. However, she showed no signs of interest in the Gospel, and then the family moved to the outskirts of Sapporo, where they had bought a house.

We kept in touch with annual New Year's cards, but that was all. About seventeen years later Tony and I took on the leadership of a church near the area where she and her husband were living. I soon visited her, renewed our friendship, and in time began inviting her to church events again. She came regularly to one of the church small groups, made friends with the Christian ladies, and then one day she confessed her faith in Jesus with much joy!

However, several months later we noticed that Mrs. Omoto seemed to be distancing herself from us and the church ladies, and she kept skipping the home group in which she had become such a happy participant. When I had the chance to ask her what the problem was, she shared with me that when she was a little girl, she was given up for adoption into a family where there were other children too. She always felt that she didn't really belong, and her heart was starved for acceptance and love.

As a young adult she met her husband. She felt that he was the one person in her life who really loved, accepted and understood her. The trouble was, he was not willing to accept her newfound faith. He was a Buddhist and Japanese society is Buddhist! He made it clear to her that he didn't want her going off in a different direction.

Mrs. Omoto couldn't face being rejected by him, so she chose her husband's conditional love over Jesus' unconditional love.

~~~~~~~~~~~~~~

Mr .Yamaguchi's mother lived with him and his wife and daughter. Although he was opposed to his mother's faith, she often took her young granddaughter to church with her. Grandmother longed for her daughter-in-law to come too, but Mrs. Yamaguchi was hardly ever free, as she helped her husband in his delivery business most Sundays. Mr. Yamaguchi had a bad temper and was extremely abusive at home, both physically and emotionally. Understandably they were all afraid of him.

When we came to lead the church where the grandmother was a member, I started to visit Mrs. Yamaguchi at times when I knew her husband wasn't at home. I was able to visit his mother openly, as he could not refuse her a visit from her church. However, he became very angry if he came home and found that his wife was also listening to our conversation.

Sometime later we held an Alpha Course at the church and on the days that she was free, Mrs. Yamaguchi secretly joined in. During the course, she joyfully gave her heart to Jesus. We encouraged her to move towards baptism, assuring her of our prayers as she shared her desire with her husband. When she mentioned to her husband that she wanted to be baptized as his mother had been, he threatened to divorce her. Mrs. Yamaguchi's position was very vulnerable. She knew that if her husband threw her out, she had little or no possibility of being able to live on her own without his financial support. She backed down and withdrew out of fear.

A retired Japanese pastor's wife who was leading the Alpha Course with us at the time wisely said, "No matter what the reason is for not obeying Jesus, it's not a good reason. I know that if she stood up to her husband, God would protect her and strengthen her faith."

Sadly, Mrs. Yamaguchi didn't know Jesus well enough to know that He would surely take care of her, so out of fear she chose to follow her abusive husband over following Jesus.

~~~~~~~~~~~~~~

Mrs. Oita lived near a little church in her neighborhood. Through attending different outreach events, she had been hearing the Gospel for a few years, but hesitated to commit herself to Jesus. Then she was found to have a tumor on the brain. Experiencing intense pain after the surgery, she said, "Suddenly I knew that the pain Jesus experienced on the cross was for me, and my heart just overflowed with gratitude and joy." Nothing could hold her back! She was born again – a new creation in Christ and eager to be baptized. It was a day of rejoicing as she shared her testimony with everyone at her baptism.

Then tragedy struck. Her adult son committed suicide. Mr. Oita called the Buddhist priest in to conduct the funeral and the subsequent rituals at the family altar. Mrs. Oita was pressured to take part in those rituals in her home – after all, this was for her son. Would she neglect to do what was felt to be culturally necessary for her own son? She compromised, and participated in the Buddhist rituals. She prayed to the spirit of her son and burned incense sticks. The result was as if cold water had been poured on her faith. Her desire to love and honor the Lord drained away.

We and other believers continued to visit her and encouraged her to return to Jesus, knowing that when believers fall back into worshiping the spirits of the dead, they lose their personal connection with God. It is as if God withdraws. They are making their choice to worship other gods, even as the Israelites did so long ago. Not long after that, Mrs. Oita's mother passed away. With many additional visits from the Buddhist priest, their home and Mrs. Oita's heart were filled with the smell of incense and worship of the spirits of the deceased.

One day when I visited her again, I reminded her that she was a child of God and that her Heavenly Father was longing for her to repent and return to Him. She looked conflicted and distressed and with great emotion asked, "Pat, why can't I do both?"

I asked her if her husband would be happy if she had another man in her life to whom she went with her problems and to whom she listened for advice. She vehemently said, "No! He would not tolerate that!" I explained to her that was just how God felt about her listening to and obeying the Buddhist priest and praying to her son's and her mother-in-law's spirit. God was jealous of her love for Him. She belonged to Him! Prayer and worship belong to Him alone!

But like the rich young man in the Gospel story, she went away sorrowful, for she chose her earthly relationships above her relationship with Jesus.

Truly it is as the Bible says "Those who cling to worthless idols turn away from God's love for them" (Jonah 2:8).

~~~~~~~~~~~~

Mrs. Suzuki had been attending a little rural church for a few years but remained uncommitted. However, when her little son died suddenly at six months, grief overwhelmed her and she started seeking answers. She went to the Buddhist priest and asked him where the spirit of her son was. He gave her a complicated answer, one that would require her to perform a lot of rituals. Not satisfied with this answer, she asked the missionary at the little church, "Can you tell me where my son is now?"

"Yes. He has gone back to the Father who gave him life in the first place," replied the missionary.

"Then I will believe in this God so that I can go there too," said Mrs. Suzuki. From that time on she sought the Lord with all her heart and she found Him!

She wanted to get baptized, but her husband threatened divorce if she went through with it. So she faithfully went to church, joined in with the witness of the church, and served her husband selflessly, hoping to draw him to Jesus too. At last, after seventeen years, she said to him one day, "I have waited long enough for you. Now I am going to be baptized even if you reject me. I love Jesus more than life itself."

Perhaps her husband realized he would be the loser if he divorced his wife, so he switched to ridiculing her. Many times he mocked his wife's faith in the presence of others. Mrs. Suzuki would look at him without animosity. Her faith was unwavering, and she became a pillar of the local church. Whenever she prayed we felt that she was lifting us right to Heaven!

Mr. Suzuki was an English teacher at a local university. Tony taught him English and Mr. Suzuki helped Tony improve his Japanese language skills. During the years they spent teaching each other they developed a friendly relationship, but Mr. Suzuki refused to consider the Gospel message.

Years later, Mr. Suzuki became seriously ill and was hospitalized. Just three weeks before he died, with much joy and peace he received the grace of God to repent and believe in His Son Jesus. From his hospital bed he acknowledged that it was the example of his wife's unwavering faith that had softened his resistant heart to make the choice to receive Jesus as his Savior.

~~~~~~~~~~~~~~

In Japan many husbands threaten their wives with divorce if they get baptized. Often the wives' choice to follow Jesus comes at great cost.

When you have a difficult choice to make that may conflict with your faith in Jesus Christ, remember that the promise of Scripture is sure: "...the one who trusts in him will never be put to shame" (1 Peter 2:6).

13. FORGIVENESS BRINGS HEALING

Tony

Bear with each other and forgive whatever grievances
you may have against one another.
- Colossians 3:13

It was February in Sapporo and the snow lay deep on the ground. A lady in a small car with her four-year-old daughter got stuck in the snow approaching the apartment block in which Pat and I were living. Despite much revving of the engine, she made no progress. We went out to help her and managed to push the car along to her parking bay. Thus began our acquaintance with Hikari, a single mother, and her shy little daughter Emma.

Keen to make the most of our new connection, we invited her to join an English class at the church. Much to our surprise, Hikari said she wasn't really interested in English, but would like to study the Bible. We were always on the lookout for people who had a desire to study the Bible, but experience told us it was better to wait patiently for an opportunity after a friendship had been established. Time is needed for building trust. People are often wary of what type of conditions and expectations there would be if they committed themselves to a Bible study. In addition, especially if the church is near their home, they fear that if the relationship does not go well, there would be no place to hide. There would be no way to politely avoid meeting each other, possibly causing embarrassment.

Our relationship with Hikari blossomed as Pat met weekly with her to study the Bible. She also started to attend church meetings with her little daughter. Hikari was reading the Bible avidly and growing in her understanding in leaps and bounds. She also shared with us that she had come to live in our apartment block because she was running away from her abusive father, with whom she and her daughter had been living after her divorce.

Soon after Hikari put her faith in Jesus Christ, we suggested that we start praying for her father. "No way," she said. "He doesn't even know where I am, and I don't want anything to do with him anymore." We just encouraged her with Jesus' words to pray for our enemies, and slowly she began to agree to pray for him. "Anyway, my father will never believe," she said. "He is very stubborn."

One day Hikari asked me to give her a hand to collect some of her furniture and belongings stored at her father's house. I was surprised that on first impression Mr. Yamaguchi seemed quite a reasonable man. However, there was obviously tension between them. As I established a bit of a relationship with her father that day, Hikari agreed to let me invite him to a church Christmas event. This was a big step for both of them.

As Hikari grew in her faith, her heart softened somewhat towards her father. She realized that as Jesus had forgiven her, she needed to forgive her father too. As she obeyed the Lord in this, their relationship improved. Hikari was baptized as a believer, and then some months later we left the church to return to Canada for home assignment. A young Japanese pastor was appointed to take over the leadership.

One day, after we had again returned to Japan and were leading a church in a different area of Sapporo, Pat was crossing the parking area of a hardware store when a man called out, "Mrs. Pat!" It was Hikari's father Mr. Yamaguchi, whom we had not seen for nearly two years. His house was only a short distance by car from the church where we were now serving. At

Pat's invitation, he said he would come to church one day. Such a response cannot always be taken literally, but Mr. Yamaguchi did come, and he became a regular attender. I started to do Bible studies with him during the week as he was retired. He began to feel at home with the other people in the church and became involved with some maintenance work as well.

During some of the studies I had spoken about not worshipping at the Buddhist altar, which many Japanese people have in their homes and where they pray to the spirits of their deceased ancestors. Mr. Yamaguchi struggled with the concept that Christians pray only to the one true God. He felt it was disloyal and disrespectful to his forebears not to perform the Buddhist rites. He also knew his relatives would not look favourably upon him as the eldest son should he not perform his duties of prayer and offerings to their ancestors. Another problem was that he had spent the equivalent of US$20,000 to purchase the altar. The Buddhist priest had said that because of certain past misfortunes in Mr. Yamaguchi's family, he needed to buy an expensive altar to appease the ancestors. I could see this might be a stumbling block to his coming to true faith. However, we pressed on with the Bible studies.

It was during an Alpha Course at the church that Mr. Yamaguchi confessed Jesus as his Lord and Saviour. One day Mr. Yamaguchi said he wanted to be baptized. I asked him about his butsudan (Buddhist altar). He looked at me in surprise and said, "Oh that? I burnt it." I nearly fell off my chair! He explained that he and his daughter had discussed the problem together and, after praying, they had gone to a plot of ground he was renting to grow vegetables. There they chopped up the altar and burned it. He was no longer afraid that the spirits of the ancestors could harm him or his extended family. Now he was trusting Jesus to protect them. What a wonderful, God-honoring act of faith by a new believer! Not only that, but he and his daughter were now also united as children of God. Forgiveness had brought healing.

Just prior to this time, another man, Mr. Ogawa, had joined the weekly Bible studies. Although I had also spoken to him about the issue of worship at the butsudan, it remained a problem to him. However, Mr. Ogawa was really moved and convicted when he heard Mr. Yamaguchi's testimony at his baptism. At the next Bible study, Mr. Ogawa eagerly quizzed Mr. Yamaguchi for more details about his handling of the butsudan issue. As a result, Mr. Ogawa went home and discussed the matter with his backslidden Christian wife. They, too, got rid of the Buddhist altar in their home prior to his baptism. Mr. Yamaguchi was so pleased that his testimony had helped another believer in taking a step of faith.

Truly, "those who cling to worthless idols forfeit the grace that could be theirs" (Jonah 2:8). Conversely, those who turn to worship the living God receive blessing upon blessing and enjoy fellowship with Him.

I remember looking over the faces of the congregation on the day of Mr. Yamaguchi's baptism. There in a row sat sixty-five-year-old Mr. Yamaguchi, his daughter Hikari and his little granddaughter Emma. They were beaming with joy! I felt tears of thankfulness come to my eyes at the wonderful way God had brought forgiveness and reconciliation to this family. He had filled their hearts with peace, joy and love for each other and for God Himself. They were a family together with God as their Father.

Have you experienced the power of forgiveness in your life? As we forgive one another, Satan loses his grip on us, and God frees us to do the good works that He has planned for us to do.

14. TAKE OFF YOUR SHOES

Tony

I have become all things to all people so that
by all possible means I might save some.
- 1 Corinthians 9:22

"Hurry up! Lie down on the bed," the doctor in the emergency room at a Vancouver hospital ordered. As I, Tony, started taking my shoes off, the doctor said impatiently, "Don't worry about that now – lie down!" Still, much to his consternation, I hastily took my shoes off before lying down on the bed. After a brief examination, I was rushed upstairs to the operating room to have three stents inserted into my arteries as there was no time for a bypass operation. I had just had a serious heart attack. After the procedure the doctor told my anxious wife that it was touch and go. Five more stents were inserted three months later, making a total of eight. I wondered whether my body might set off the alarms when going through an airport security check!

Why did I feel I had to take off my shoes while the doctor was waiting impatiently for me? You see, we had worked in Japan as missionaries for many years. It would be unthinkable for a Japanese person to lie on a bed with shoes on, and so it was for me too. Even though I was already retired and I am not Japanese, some of the culture has become part of who I am.

When we first arrived in Japan in 1972, the customs seemed strange and different. Taking off one's shoes and putting on slippers when entering homes, changing into other slippers to go to the washroom and changing back into the original slippers, took a lot of concentration! Then there were hours of practicing picking up beans with chopsticks so we could eat without dropping our food and embarrassing our Japanese friends. As time went on, these and many other customs began to feel normal to us as foreigners living in Japan. Over the years we assimilated something of the Japanese culture, and this has changed our thinking and behavior.

Hudson Taylor, the founder of OMF International (formerly China Inland Mission), found that after he altered his clothes and hairstyle to identify with the Chinese people, he had a more attentive audience when sharing the Gospel. Paul, the New Testament missionary, was willing to become all things to all people to win some to Christ. In modern Japan a foreigner doesn't have to change their hairstyle or style of clothes, but we must change many behavioral patterns so as not to cause unnecessary offence or be a distraction as we share the Gospel.

The Japanese bath

Just when we thought we could explain Japanese bathing procedures to visitors from abroad, our instructions once backfired because we left out one important detail.

Taking a bath is something Japanese families look forward to. Everyone enjoys a wonderfully relaxing soak in the tub. Each family member in turn uses the same tubful of water, which remains clean because all soaping, shampooing, dousing and rinsing is done outside the tub. The soapy water runs down the drain in the middle of the tiled floor. Traditionally the father goes in first, but if there is a guest, the guest bathes first.

There was no hot water system in our rented house, so the bath was filled with cold water which was then heated with a kerosene stove. This process could take an hour or more. When the bath was ready on that day, we gave careful instructions to our guest. He seemed a bit bewildered at being told how to bathe, but graciously nodded his head and went into the bathroom. However, we had left out one small detail in our explanation – you don't pull the plug after your bath!

Our guest, of course, did what he would do in his own country. He pulled the plug when he had finished. That rendered our careful explanation meaningless. It would take too long to refill the tub and heat the water, so there were some disappointed people in our family that day when they found there was to be no bath. We let him save face by not commenting on it. Hopefully someone would give him better instructions the next time!

The communal neighborhood bath centers in Japan were big enough to allow ten or more people to soak at a time and were wonderful places to connect with neighbors. These days the same enjoyment is found in larger spas. Sitting in hot water up to your neck during the cold winter months melts away all the stress of the day. The Japanese bath is one of the things I have missed the most since leaving Japan, especially during our cold Canadian winters. (By the way, a person who has a tattoo on their body is not permitted to enter a Japanese communal bath. That's the rule!)

However, there are more difficult parts of adjusting to the culture, namely, adjusting to the Japanese worldview.

Guessing – Sassuru

Sassuru is the art or skill of guessing, presuming, or coming to understand the intended meaning of a conversation without having it spelled out. This is a very difficult skill for us foreigners to learn. A Japanese university graduate went to a western country to study English to prepare for an overseas assignment. I asked him what was most difficult for him during his training. Was it speaking English? The climate? The food?

He replied that it was the frustration he felt at having to explain everything down to the last syllable before people understood what he was saying. Why couldn't they get the intent of his communication without his having to literally spell it out to the last word? He found that embarrassing and exhausting. These people were adults, not children, so they should have been able to understand, he maintained. That's when he told me about sassuru, but I'm afraid he had to spell it out to the last syllable before I understood what he meant!

Reading the air – Kuuki wo Yomu

This is closely linked to sassuru but it is a little different. People who are not good at "reading the air" are called KY (kuuki wo yomenai) – literally someone who cannot read the air (atmosphere). "Reading the air" involves taking note of a person's body language, or the tension felt at the time of the conversation, or the type of words used in talking about the item under review. All aspects contain a hint of a person's opinion. Even words not spoken can contain a clear expression of opinion. Thus a certain conclusion is conveyed to those who are able to "read the air." Maybe the closest English equivalent to that would be "reading between the lines."

I once attended a special church deacons' meeting where there was a problem concerning money that was missing. The man in question, Mr. A, was not present at the meeting. Listening very carefully, I checked off each name one by one as those present spoke. One person said it was unfortunately incomprehensible how the amount of money came to be missing, but there was no definite proof that Mr. A had taken the money. Another said Mr. A had responsibility for the safekeeping of the money, but there were other people who could also have had access to the place where the money was kept. Another person said he noticed that Mr. A had been working alone after others had left, so he did have an opportunity, but he had always been a faithful treasurer. Another said proper controls had been put in place, so it was unimaginable how the money could have gone missing. Someone who had access to the money must have taken it.

As each person spoke, I came to the conclusion that Mr. A was innocent and, being the last person to speak, I said so. The group of six Japanese people looked at me in startled disbelief, as if to say, "Have you been sleeping during the entire meeting?" After everyone had gone, an elderly deacon explained to me that although no one had said directly that Mr. A was guilty, each person had added color to the issue through their comments, and all the colors were dark. Only mine was light! Therefore the consensus among the group was that Mr. A must have taken the money. I had to reflect on that for a long time. I had definitely been KY! I learned to read from books when I went to school but had never been taught to read the air!

Public and private opinions – tatemae and honne

These characteristics of the Japanese culture are extremely difficult for a foreigner to distinguish. At first glance it appears to be an issue of pretence and reality, but it is a principle practised to maintain harmony in the public place. Truth is only discussed behind closed doors with "family" – those who belong to the inside group. Tatemae and honne are actually difficult even for some Japanese, because in order to keep the harmony of the group they belong to, they are often not free to express their true opinions.

Many foreigners regard tatemae and honne as lies and truth, but this simple deduction would be wrong. The more knowledge and understanding we acquired while living in Japan, the more we came to understand the courtesies necessary to maintain harmonious relationships between people. The greater the level of trust between people, the more likely a person will be to hear honne rather than tatemae talk.

I remember a combined pastors' and missionaries' meeting where one of the missionaries gave a farewell testimony as she was leaving Japan to pursue a ministry in her home country. The pastor who was leading the meeting asked, "Ms. Brown, what was most difficult for you in your service in Japan?" She replied without hesitation, "honne and tatemae."

"Well," said the leader, "you did very well, and we appreciate the deep understanding you have of the Japanese culture."

The missionary quickly retorted, "Is that honne or tatemae?" Everyone laughed because that was the point. No one knew, except those on the inside, whether what the leader had said was honne or tatemae. Was it genuine or was it mere etiquette? We had our suspicions!

In a culture that puts such a high value on harmony, we foreigners have to learn to appreciate the need for tatemae and honne. However, as Christians we have to graciously move towards sharing our honne with people, all the while remembering that truth without grace can be offensive and hurtful. The best way to communicate is with grace and truth, which Jesus exemplified perfectly to us (John 1:14).

Influencing others

A senior missionary once told me that if you want to influence a Japanese leader you have to come gently alongside rather than attempt a head-on approach. He said it is like a small tug boat trying to make a large cargo vessel change its course. A head-on approach would not work, but a gentle bump on the side may result in the larger vessel changing direction. During our time in Japan we found this to be very helpful advice.

I remember once suggesting to a pastor that we do some teaching on fasting and prayer. He was fine with prayer, but said that they didn't usually practise fasting in Japan. I was about to remind him of Matthew chapter 6 when I remembered the earlier advice, so I said no more. Two weeks later the pastor said he had been reading up on fasting and, after praying about it, was now convinced that we should teach about prayer and fasting. His conviction carried weight among other pastors in the same church organization and as a result, several others began to emphasize the blessing of praying with fasting in their teaching.

Some general differences in ministry thinking

An often-encountered difference between foreign missionaries and Japanese church leaders concerns the roles of the pastor and the missionary. By and large, Japanese pastors view their role as shepherds of the flock of God under their care. This is a Biblical view of the role of a pastor which they rightly take seriously. The shepherd should know where his sheep are so he can give an explanation when asked about a believer's absence from worship, for example, or have knowledge to be able to pray appropriately for the members of his flock. Should the pastor not know the reason for a person's absence, it could be thought that either the person has disrespectfully not informed the pastor, or that the pastor has not bothered to inquire, which might show a lack of care by the shepherd.

On the other hand, missionary church leaders generally view their role more as being commissioned to equip the saints for ministry. The Church is the Body of Christ, so each member must be trained to do their part in building up the Body. This is also a Biblical view. These different emphases of the same role can cause tension, but with respect and patience, both sides can end up with a better understanding and appreciation of a church leader's role and make some adjustments to their own way of leading the flock of God.

Having been in Japan for several years, I was used to the fact that one should let one's pastor know if one is not going to be in church on a Sunday. When I went to South Africa on home assignment, I told my pastor every time I would be preaching elsewhere. One day my pastor said, "Look, Tony, I don't need to know what you are doing on Sundays. You don't have to let me know!" I realized that I had become very Japanese in my thinking.

Harmony above all else

Japan is a highly organized, efficiently run, homogenous society. If you stay on the rails by doing the culturally acceptable thing there should be no problem – or perhaps only a minimum amount of trouble. However, if you step off the rails and do something different from what is expected of you in any given situation, there is bound to be trouble. People feel comfortable when everyone stays on track by doing the right and acceptable thing, thereby maintaining harmony.

This can be a huge problem for people considering the Christian faith. It also poses a problem for our Japanese brothers and sisters in Christ, because Jesus calls us to come and follow Him, and His ways are often very different from those of the society we live in. Actually this is true in every culture. However, sometimes as foreigners we cannot sufficiently empathize with our Japanese brothers and sisters as to the extent of the dilemma they face in making decisions to follow Christ rather than the crowd. The "crowd" could be their family, or their place of employment, or any small group to which they belong. Whereas in western cultures we encourage people to follow their personal convictions, to the average Japanese those words are just a tatemae way of encouraging selfishness. Japanese people always seriously consider how their personal conduct may affect their groups. No decisions are made without consideration of the groups to which they belong. As much as possible, the groups in which a person participates should not only be consulted first, but also be in agreement with their proposed action. This is viewed as not causing trouble.

It has been a privilege and a struggle for us to grapple with this problem with fellow missionaries and our Japanese brothers and sisters who wish to follow the call of Christ in a society where the need for harmony supersedes everything else.

Of course there are many other things we learned from living in Japan. We cannot list the number of lessons we have learned under the gracious and patient teaching of our Japanese friends. We are still learning to be "a Japanese to the Japanese" in order to win them to Christ.

Is there someone whose lifestyle or thinking you need to adjust to in order to smooth the way to share Christ with them? May the Lord help you to do so!

15. RFA FOR JESUS

Tony

Each one should use whatever gift he has received to serve others, faithfully administering God's grace in its various forms.
- 1 Peter 4:10

In earlier days when Christians offered themselves for missionary work, the offer was open-ended and usually thought to be for life. These days it would be correct to say that most long-term missionaries have had a short-term experience somewhere before they made their long-term commitment. While we were missionaries in Japan, it was our privilege to welcome many short-term teams. Over the years we had teams and individuals from churches in Canada, Singapore, England, the USA, and most frequently from a church in Hong Kong. From each of these countries, some short-termers have proceeded to become long-term missionaries. Many of the short-termers gave up their annual holiday to share the love of Jesus with the Japanese people. Every team was used by God in unique ways in outreach, as well as in demonstrating to the local Japanese believers a heart for the world and a desire to share the Gospel.

In one of the churches we were leading, we welcomed a short-term team almost every summer. In the team debriefings, one of the most frequent comments was that they wished they could have spent more time working together with the Japanese believers. We would have liked to see that too, but we felt that by the time summer came, the local Christians who served so faithfully in the church throughout the year deserved a break.

That was where the summer teams came in. They afforded the possibility of doing various outreach events, and distributing Gospel flyers in our immediate neighborhood and beyond to advertise our church programs. However, we always prayed that the local believers would catch the vision and, of their own volition, join the summer teams.

After a few years, things began to change. The believers wanted to be actively involved in the summer outreach programs. They encouraged the short-term teams by helping with tract distribution, helping translate the team's testimonies into Japanese, and providing homestays for them. This also became an opportunity to be a witness to the unbelieving spouses and children. One year, the young Japanese believers took it upon themselves to deliver the main message at all the outreach events by spending hours practicing the very meaningful drama "The Redeemer." They not only presented it at their own church but also at the outreach event of a smaller country church.

Through the short-term teams, the passion for sharing the good news of Jesus was ignited. At least two of the young people from the church went into mission work after their experience with the summer teams.

A lot of preparation is required before a team arrives. The sending church or organization has the responsibility of selecting suitable candidates who have a desire to serve. We had one requirement and that was RFA – Ready For Anything! Unrealistic expectations can ruin a summer. The teams from the church in Hong Kong exemplified the RFA qualification. One year they were asked by the advisor pastor of the church to make a huge banner to advertise an upcoming Alpha Course. This is a course designed to introduce people to Jesus and lead them to faith. None of the team members had ever done anything like this before, and it proved to be very difficult. One lady quietly said to me, "It's a pity the pastor didn't tell us this was needed ahead of time. We could have had it made in Hong Kong very inexpensively and brought a ready-made one with us!" But we heard no complaints as we worked together to perfect the banner. The huge banner was hung up outside on the front of the church for all passers-by to see. As far as we know no one came "off the street" to the Alpha course, but the four people who attended, all made professions of faith – an abundant harvest indeed!

Soon after the tsunami devastated the north east coastal region of Japan on March 11, 2011, many opportunities arose to give assistance, and short-term teams played an invaluable role in showing love and practical care for those whose lives had been so tragically changed that day.

At that time OMF was able to put up a pre-fabricated drop-in center in the small town of Yamada that had been devastated by the tsunami. The center was called Ippo Ippo, which means step by step. It proved to be a place where many found healing and hope, step by step.

A young nurse, Yuka, had been seconded by the hospital where she worked to help at the over-stretched hospital on the coast. From dealing every day with the stories of tragic deaths, the frantic faces of people looking for loved ones, and caring for the wounded, she began to crumble inside. She would come to the drop-in center daily and pour out her heart to the Christian workers there and receive prayer. Ippo Ippo became her place to be renewed for another day's work. She had heard the Gospel as a young exchange student in England and had believed, but she never followed through when she returned to Japan. When we were there with a short-term team from Hong Kong, Yuka still came a few times a week to talk with the team members, and was deeply encouraged by the rich fellowship they offered her. Yuka was baptized at Christmas that year. The following summer, through her introduction, we led a team from the same church in Hong Kong for two weeks of summer evangelism at the church where Yuka is a member!

That summer, in true RFA style, the team agreed to weed the church's large burial plot on the outskirts of the town. In a culture where ancestor worship is attached to the custom of visiting graves, it is important for the churches to have their own burial plot for the ashes of the deceased Christians and their families. In this way they could cut their ties with the Buddhist temples where the ashes would otherwise be stored. We were asked to help clean the site by cutting the grass, weeding and tidying up in preparation for the summer visitors. We were warned there would be insects, so we wore gloves, long sleeves and caps. In the over 30 degrees Celsius heat, the guys cut the grass while the ladies raked it into piles. Suddenly shouts of alarm erupted. People started running in all directions. One man and his wife from the church jumped into their car for refuge. Someone had disturbed a hornet's nest and the hornets sent out an attack party to ward off the intruders! Three people suffered painful stings. The rest of us offered our sympathies, relieved that we ourselves had been spared. Someone went to the drugstore to get medication for the stings. After all, being a RFA team, they valiantly completed their task. I was told that eating ice cream later that day lessened the pain somewhat!

Sometimes we had to contend with more than the heat. One day, while walking around handing out flyers to people we met, or putting them into mail boxes, one of the team members looked up to see an angry dog darting towards her. There was no escape for her, so she just shouted out "Father!" The growling dog suddenly stopped and quietened down. The dog had stopped short even though its leash was not yet fully extended! God was protecting His own. However, even after her narrow escape, her heart was in her mouth and her legs felt like they had turned to jelly.

Weeding, trimming trees (almost destroying one!), hand massaging, conducting cooking classes, distributing flyers in the summer heat, teaching English, singing, performing dramas, making balloon animals, all with warm, open hearts and smiles brought many people under the sound of the Gospel, many for the first time. We thank the Lord for every short-term team that came! They were an encouragement to the local Christians and were themselves blessed serving the Lord in Japan.

Joining a short-term mission team is often a life-changing experience. Why not investigate it for yourself? If you have a heart to serve and are RFA, you are never too young or too old to make an impact for the Gospel. If you are interested, check out the OMF website at OMF.org, and trust the Lord to lead you.

16. A MAJOR CHALLENGE TO FAITH

Tony

*See, I lay a stone in Zion, a chosen and precious cornerstone,
and the one who trusts in Him will never be put to shame.*
- 1 Peter 2:6

"On what topic will you be writing your thesis?" my seminary professor asked.

"Church planting in Japan," I replied, thinking that I could draw on my missionary experience to make for a not-too-stressful study.

"Hmmm," the professor mused. "By the way, what do you think is the main reason why so few Japanese come to Christ?"

"It's difficult to say, but probably the tie to the worship of the ancestral spirits is a major hindrance." I ventured to reply.

"That is what I want you to write about – ancestor worship in Japan," he announced.

"But I know so little about that subject," I protested. However, a year later, by the grace of God, I completed my thesis for a Master of Ministry degree.

Is ancestor worship really worship of the deceased person's spirit, or is it more about honoring and remembering the deceased? Is this custom similar to what Western people do when they place flowers on the grave of a loved one?

At first glance these two customs appear to be similar. As foreigners, we need to dig deep to be able to speak to the heart of those who wish to honor and revere their ancestors, whom they regard as still actively involved in the family. What does praying to the spirits, lighting incense sticks, and making offerings to the spirits of ancestors represent? Is honoring their ancestors merely showing respect, or is it worship? To show respect and honor for a person is compatible with Scripture, but worship (which includes prayer) is due to God alone. "You shall have no other gods before me" (Exodus 20:1).

During our first church planting assignment in the city of Sapporo, we became quite friendly with the family next door. They allowed their children to attend Sunday school, including their oldest son Jun, who was about eleven years of age. During one summer vacation Jun attended a children's Christian camp, where he heard and responded to the Gospel.

A day or two after the camp ended, I was holding a Bible study in our home when the doorbell rang. The young boy at the door asked me to come down to the river where some local children had been playing. I replied that I was busy and would join them later. However, the boy didn't leave. I looked at him more closely and noticed that he looked distraught. He said Jun had dived into the river and hadn't resurfaced! I immediately called out to the man with whom I was studying that there was an emergency, and ran down to the river with the boy.

There I found a group of young boys staring at the water. The flow wasn't strong and I shouted for them to help me look for their missing friend, but nobody moved. I jumped in and was soon joined by my wife Pat. After what seemed a long time, we discovered Jun submerged in the water. We applied artificial respiration as best we could, while a neighbor called an ambulance, but it was too late. Jun had drowned.

The boys later told me they were afraid to go into the water to look for Jun because they thought that a spirit might pull them in too. The devastated family was thankful for our rescue attempt, but subsequently withdrew from all contact with the church. Despite our offer to conduct a Christian funeral for Jun, they held a Buddhist funeral. After that, it seemed as though a thick, dark curtain had been lowered between them and the church. None of their other children attended Sunday school again. Soon an enormous Buddhist altar filled the family's sitting room and each day Jun's family would pray to their son's spirit.

A Christian Japanese author lists the main features of the practice of ancestor worship as:

1. Providing an origin for the existence of the household which has the family's well-being at heart.

2. Demanding absolute respect for the ancestors of one's household, which is binding on all members.

3. Regarding the ancestors as the wellspring from which the family line derives.

4. Regarding ancestors as the ultimate guarantors of the family's well-being down through the generations.

5. Teaching that the spirits of ancestors grow wrathful if not properly revered.

6. Maintaining that the blessings upon the household are derived from the spirits of the ancestors.

Is it any wonder that the vast majority who inquire about Christianity ask, "If I become a Christian, can I still worship at the Buddhist altar?" They feel they owe their ancestors a debt of gratitude, which is based on a strong concept of filial piety. It is understandable that a person who does not believe in an eternal, sovereign God would baulk at offending one's own household members by not worshipping their ancestors.

Apart from prayer, what should the Church do to overcome this seemingly insurmountable problem? Is there an acceptable, compassionate way through this dilemma? How have Christians down through the ages sought to resolve this?

To gain some insight, I sent out 172 questionnaires to Japanese pastors and missionaries of various denominations who had worked in Japan for longer than four years. Nineteen questions were posed and I received 114 replies. The overwhelming response was that the practice of ancestor worship is a major problem to the Christian Church in Japan. Sadly and surprisingly, however, there was quite a divergence of opinion on how to practically deal with the problem.

Some thought-provoking suggestions were made:

1. The Creator God could be thought of as humankind's first ancestor. He is worthy to be worshiped because He is divine. Adam could be regarded as our second ancestor but he, like the rest of humankind, is mortal and therefore not worthy of worship. Neither Adam nor any other succeeding mortal being, neither angels nor any other created being is worthy to be worshiped. A person may be worthy of respect and honor but definitely not of worship.

2. Christianize the Buddhist altar by placing a cross on the top with Bible verses relating to the resurrection of Jesus. Prayers could be made to God. A reading of the names of the household ancestors could be done, giving thanks to God for His provision and care for the family through the years.

   However, it was thought that this approach would be difficult to distinguish from the rituals performed at the Buddhist altar, which might then lead to confusion in the minds of non-Christians.

3. Should Christians even attend a Buddhist funeral? Their absence would avoid confrontation, but would it be a testimony to God's love and grace? Would it not be better to attend the funeral and help with neutral practical

matters while abstaining from any act of worship of the deceased person's spirit? Christians could take the opportunity to speak well of the deceased person and offer words of sympathy to the bereaved. That would keep the door open for future opportunities to witness to the family and friends.

Thankfully, the Lord has established His Church in Japan through which the Gospel is proclaimed. The words and actions of believers, combined with their warm, joyful fellowship, form a powerful witness.

Yoko was a young wife who was profoundly moved when she attended her mother-in-law's Christian funeral. Neither she nor her husband were believers, so she was amazed when people sang hymns and conducted a joyful celebration of her mother-in-law's life. Yoko was so impressed by the difference between a Christian funeral and a Buddhist one, she started attending a local church. She became a believer and raised her four children as Christians, despite her husband's opposition. Later in life, when he became seriously ill, Yoko's husband's heart softened and in time he also believed in Jesus. Yoko's mother-in-law did not see her son or Yoko and their children become Christians before she died. Yet the Lord used her funeral to draw them all to faith. The celebration of her faithful life brought forth an abundant harvest.

More than ninety-five percent of pastors and missionaries I polled regarded the worship of the spirits of ancestors as a major concern confronting the Church in Japan.

What answer do you give to the inquirer who asks, "If I become a Christian, can I still worship/honor my ancestors?" Both parties realize that if the answer given is negative, further inquiry will end because of the fear of family opposition. So what answer can be given?

We usually said, "The answer will come later, but first find out who Jesus is and let Him teach you. Then you can make your decision."

Some people rejected our invitation to study the Bible to find the answer. Others agreed to do a limited time of study, which sometimes was extended, leading to faith. Their question then became, "How can I effectively share Jesus with my family and friends?"

When Hiroko came to believe in Jesus, her husband refused to allow her to be baptized. He was concerned that her baptism would complicate relationships within his family, especially when they gathered for family occasions at his parents' home. At those times each family member was expected to pay their respect to the ancestors by bowing, offering a prayer and lighting incense at the family altar. Hiroko's husband warned her not to embarrass him when the extended family gathered that first New Year after she had believed.

When it was Hiroko's turn to step forward, she nervously stood in front of the Buddhist altar. As a Christian she wanted to honor God because He alone is worthy of worship. Hiroko just stood motionless at the altar, weeping. She did not offer a prayer to the spirits of the ancestors nor light an incense stick. She returned to her seat feeling a failure. Her husband was smouldering with fury because he felt his wife had disgraced him. Angrily he berated her in front of the whole family.

Upon their return home, Hiroko shared her experience with her church family. With tears coursing down her cheeks, she recounted how she felt she had not given a clear testimony of her faith and had not explained what she believed. Her husband was still furious. However, her mother-in-law had told her, "If I believed my religion as strongly as you believe yours, I think I would be happy."

Many difficult years followed in their married life, but God was at work. Her husband started to attend church with Hiroko and eventually believed and was baptized. Later he even became a devoted church deacon. During his baptismal testimony he said it was his wife's unwavering obedience to the Lord that convinced him to seek God for himself.

There are some successes but unfortunately there are many failures too. Often believers succumb to society's pressure to conform and compromise their faith when it comes to taking a stand against the worship of the spirits of the ancestors.

Would you pray that many Japanese will come to know the "chosen and precious Cornerstone" and experience that all those who put their trust in Him will never be put to shame?

**Look for Tony's first book of stories
wherever you buy books:**

ebook 978-1775146216
paperback 978-1775146209

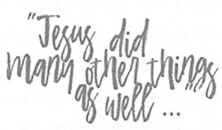

SHORT STORIES OUT OF JAPAN

TONY SCHMIDT

Milton Keynes UK
Ingram Content Group UK Ltd.
UKHW051050271123
433333UK00012B/230